The Library of Small Ecosystems™

The Ecosystem of a
Grassy Field

Elaine Pascoe   Photography by **Dwight Kuhn**

The Rosen Publishing Group's
PowerKids Press™
New York

Published in 2003 by The Rosen Publishing Group, Inc.
29 East 21st Street, New York, NY 10010

First Edition

Editor: Nancy MacDonell Smith
Book Design: Michael J. Caroleo

Photo Credits: Photos © Dwight Kuhn.

Pascoe, Elaine.
The ecosystem of a grassy field / by Elaine Pascoe.— 1st ed.
    p. cm. — (The library of small ecosystems)
Includes bibliographical references (p.   ).
Summary: Simple text describes the plants and animals that inhabit a grassy field, creating an interrelated ecosystem.
ISBN 0-8239-6305-5 (lib. bdg.)
1. Grassland ecology—Juvenile literature. [1. Grassland ecology. 2. Ecology.] I. Title.
QH541.5.P7 P37 2003
577.4—dc21

                                  2001006016

Manufactured in the United States of America

Contents

The Field

Look quickly at a field, and grass is all you see. Look closely and you will see much more. A field is as busy as a city. Many kinds of plants grow among the grasses. Insects, birds, mice, deer, meadow **voles**, and other animals find food and make their homes in a field.

A field is a small **ecosystem**. An ecosystem is a community made up of living and nonliving elements. The insects, the birds, and the other living things all depend on this community to **survive**. Every part of the ecosystem has a role to play. Even the air that ruffles the grass and the soil beneath the field are important.

Top: *This meadow vole is one member of the grassy field community.*
Bottom: *Though it looks quiet, this field is as full as a big city.*

More than Grass

In spring and summer, a field is filled with blossoms. Daisies, dandelions, and other wildflowers bloom. Even grass has flowers, but the flowers of grass are so tiny that they are hard to see.

In time the flowers fade. Seeds form where the blossoms were. When the seeds are ready, they break away from the plants. Seeds scatter all over the field. They are either carried by the wind or are scattered in other ways. Some seeds are eaten by birds. However, if a seed lands in a good spot, it will **sprout**. In this way new plants grow up in a field every year.

Many different types of wildflowers grow in a field.
Inset: If this dandelion's seeds land in a good spot, new plants will sprout.

The flowers and the seeds of grasses are carried on long stalks above the plants.

In spring a grassy field is filled with dandelion flowers.

8

Lupine is one kind of wildflower that grows in a field.

A new plant sprouts from a dandelion seed.

9

Plants on the Menu

The grasses and other plants in a field are food for many different kinds of animals. Deer are among the largest visitors to a field. They usually stay hidden in the woods during the day. At dusk they come to the field to **browse**. They nibble on leaves, buds, and flowers until morning comes.

Woodchucks eat grass, clover, and other plants. Woodchucks usually feed early in the morning and late in the afternoon. Every so often a woodchuck sits up on its hind legs and looks around to check for danger. Then it goes back to eating. By the end of summer, woodchucks are very fat. They spend the winter in a deep sleep in **burrows** in the field, living off of their fat.

This woodchuck is taking a break from eating to check for danger.
Inset: *Deer come to a field at night to feed.*

Leaf Eaters and Sap Suckers

Insects find food in the grassy field, too. Some insects eat leaves. Others drink **nectar**, a sweet liquid in flowers. Still other insects suck sap from plant stems.

The **spittlebug** is a sap feeder. This little insect is smaller than your fingernail. As it feeds, the spittlebug covers itself with bubbly foam that its body makes. The foam hides the insect and keeps it from drying out in the hot sun.

A grassy field is filled with insect life. If you stop and listen on a summer day, you will hear insects humming, buzzing, and chirping all over the field.

Left: *This spittlebug is covering itself with foam.*
Right: *Once the spittlebug is covered with foam, it's hidden from danger.*

Like the woodchuck, the cottontail rabbit feeds on the grasses that grow in a field.

The grasshopper is one of the many insects that make their homes in a field. Grasshoppers make a singing sound by rubbing their wings together or by rubbing their legs against their wings.

14

Butterflies like flowers that have plenty of nectar.

15

Left: A honeybee helps plants by carrying pollen from flower to flower.

Right: An earthworm tunnels in the soil.

Helping Plants Grow

Insects and other animals come to the field for food. Many of these animals also help plants to grow. For example, when bees and butterflies feed on nectar, they carry **pollen** from flower to flower. Pollen is a powder made by the male part of the flower. Seeds begin to form when grains of pollen land on the **pistil**. The pistil is the female part at the center of the flower.

Down among the roots of the plants, earthworms tunnel through the soil. The earthworms eat dead leaves and other material. They digest these materials, breaking them down into simple parts. When the worms push out their wastes, they add **nutrients** to the soil. The grasses and other plants take up the nutrients through their roots. In this way earthworms help to keep the field green and growing.

Insect Hunters

The field holds danger for insects. **Predators** lurk in the grass, waiting to catch them.

A garden spider spins fine strands of silk from body parts called **spinnerets**. The spider weaves the silk into a sticky web stretched among the grasses. If a grasshopper wanders into the web, it is trapped. The spider rushes over and wraps the grasshopper in more silk. The spider will feed on the grasshopper later.

Not all spiders spin webs. The crab spider waits on a flower. When an insect comes to drink nectar, the crab spider grabs the insect and bites it. The crab spider's bite poisons the insect.

Ambush bugs also catch and eat insects. The ambush bug looks just like part of a plant. Insects don't see the bug until it strikes. The bug grabs insects and eats them.

Left: *This garden spider has trapped a grasshopper in a web.*

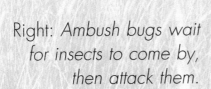

Right: *Ambush bugs wait for insects to come by, then attack them.*

This hover fly must watch out for spiders and other predators as it feeds on flower nectar.

This jumping spider has caught a deer fly. The jumping spider does not need a web to catch insects. It pounces on its prey like a cat.

20

Like the jumping spider, the crab spider does not spin a web to catch insects. Instead the crab spider waits for insects on a flower. When an insect comes to the flower to feed on nectar, the crab spider catches it.

21

Left: *This mother meadow vole is looking after her young, which are blind and hairless.*

Right: *This white-footed mouse is eating one of the blackberries that grow in a field.*

A Home at Ground Level

White-footed mice and meadow voles make their homes in the field. These animals make pathways and tunnels, above and below the ground. Mice and voles feed on leaves, seeds, and fruits such as wild raspberries.

A female vole makes a nest under a tree root at the edge of the field. The nest is lined with grass. It is a safe place for her young. The baby voles are born blind and hairless, but they grow quickly. Within 10 days they have fur and their eyes are open. In another week or two they are ready to leave the nest.

The Killdeer's Nest

The **killdeer** lays its eggs right in the middle of a field. The eggs are **camouflaged** so that predators can't see them. The speckled eggs look like stones lying on the ground. The chicks hatch in about four weeks or a little less. They are speckled, too. It takes a very sharp eye to spot them! If a fox or another predator comes near the nest, the mother killdeer springs into action. She runs away from the nest, peeping and dragging a wing as if it were broken. The fox follows her. Once she has led the fox away from the nest, the mother killdeer flies to safety.

Top: *A killdeer protects her eggs by sitting on them.* Bottom: *The eggs look like speckled stones so that even if the mother is not there to protect them, predators will have a hard time seeing them.*

These newly hatched killdeer are speckled so that predators can't see them.

The killdeer lures predators away from her nest by dragging a wing as if it were broken.

This baby killdeer is about two days old. It's still too young to fly away from danger, but its camouflage helps to protect it from predators, such as foxes.

Hunters in the Field

Foxes visit a field to hunt for mice, voles, and other small animals. These animals must be on the lookout at all times. They also need to watch for snakes, hawks, owls, and other predators. **Kestrels** often glide over the field. With its keen sight, a kestrel can see a small animal moving on the ground. Then the kestrel dives to catch its **prey**.

Predators have an important role in the community of the field. Without predators the numbers of insects and small animals that eat plants would grow too large. The plant eaters might eat all the plants! In this way, predators help to keep the ecosystem in balance.

Left: *The fox hunts small animals on the ground.*
Right: *The kestrel swoops down on its prey from the sky.*

The Grassy Field Community

From wildflowers to spiders to foxes, all the living things in a grassy field depend on one another. The plants provide food for insects, such as spittlebugs and bees, and for animals, such as woodchucks. Insects help the plants to form seeds. Earthworms improve the soil to help the plants to grow. Some of the animals that eat plants become food for spiders and larger predators, such as foxes. Predators keep the number of plant eaters in check so that the plant eaters do not eat up all the plants.

In the same way, living things everywhere depend on others to survive. A grassy field is just one of Earth's many small ecosystems.

Glossary

ambush bugs (AM-bush BUGZ) Insects that lie in wait to catch and kill other insects.

browse (BROWZ) To feed on grass or leaves by nibbling here and there.

burrows (BUR-ohz) Holes that animals dig in the ground for shelter.

camouflaged (KA-muh-flajd) Hidden by a pattern that matches the background.

ecosystem (EE-koh-sis-tehm) A community of living things and the surroundings, such as air, soil, and water, in which they live.

kestrels (KEHS-trulz) Small birds of prey, also called sparrow hawks, that are members of the same family as falcons.

killdeer (KIHL-deer) A bird that nests on the ground in open fields.

nectar (NEK-tur) A sugary liquid in the center of a flower.

nutrients (NOO-tree-ints) Anything that a living thing needs to live and to grow.

pistil (PIS-tuhl) The female part of a flower.

pollen (PAH-lin) A powder that comes from the male part of a flower.

predators (PREH-duh-terz) Animals that catch and eat other animals.

prey (PRAY) An animal that is caught and eaten by another animal.

spinnerets (spih-nuh-REHTS) Parts of a spider's body that make silk.

spittlebug (SPIH-tul-bug) A small insect that feeds on sap and covers itself with foam.

sprout (SPROWT) To begin to grow.

survive (sur-VYV) To stay alive.

voles (VOHLZ) Small animals that are members of the same family as mice.

Index

A
ambush bugs, 18

B
burrows, 11

C
camouflaged, 24

E
earthworms, 17, 30
eggs, 24

I
insects, 12, 17–18,
    29–30

K
kestrel(s), 29
killdeer, 24

N
nectar, 12, 17–18
nutrients, 17

P
pistil, 17
pollen, 17
predator(s), 18, 24,
    29–30
prey, 29

S
seeds, 6, 17, 23, 30
soil, 5, 30
spider(s), 18, 30
spinnerets, 18
spittlebug, 12, 30

V
vole(s), 5, 23, 29

W
wildflowers, 6, 30
woodchuck(s), 11, 30

Web Sites

Due to the changing nature of Internet links, PowerKids Press has developed an online list of Web sites related to the subject of this book. This site is updated regularly. Please use this link to access the list:
www.powerkidslinks.com/lse/grasseco/